T0018726

# STRONG
## AS HELL

**Celebrate Your Power, Supercharge
Your Resilience and Lift Your Vibe**

MARIA MEDEIROS

summersdale

YOU ARE STRONG AS HELL

Compiled by Maria Medeiros

An Hachette UK Company
www.hachette.co.uk

Summersdale Publishers Ltd
Part of Octopus Publishing Group Limited
Carmelite House
50 Victoria Embankment
LONDON
EC4Y 0DZ
UK

www.summersdale.com

Printed and bound in China

ISBN: 978-1-80007-344-9

Substantial discounts on bulk quantities of Summersdale books are available to corporations, professional associations and other organizations. For details contact general enquiries: telephone: +44 (0) 1243 771107 or email: enquiries@summersdale.com.

TO .................................

FROM .............................

# JUST BE YOURSELF, THERE IS NO ONE BETTER.

TAYLOR SWIFT

A strong
woman looks a
challenge dead in
the eye and gives
it a wink.

GINA CAREY

**STRONG WOMEN DON'T HAVE ATTITUDES — WE HAVE STANDARDS AND BOUNDARIES**

# A WOMAN WITH A VOICE IS BY DEFINITION A STRONG WOMAN.

MELINDA GATES

YOU
MUST KNOW
THAT YOU
CAN DO THIS.
YOU ARE
STRONG.

HEATHER A. STILLUFSEN

Women are like teabags. We don't know our true strength until we are in hot water.

ELEANOR ROOSEVELT

YOU ARE
STRONGER
THAN YOU
KNOW

I AM STRONG.
YOU WILL NOT
DETERMINE
MY STORY.
I WILL.

AMY SCHUMER

EVERYTHING
IS WITHIN YOUR
POWER, AND
YOUR POWER IS
WITHIN YOU.

JANICE TRACHTMAN

# A STRONG WOMAN STANDS UP FOR HERSELF.

# A STRONGER WOMAN STANDS UP FOR ALL AROUND HER

I LIKE FEELING
STRONG. IT KEEPS
MY MENTAL
FLOOR HIGHER.

P!NK

# THERE IS NO LIMIT TO WHAT WE, AS WOMEN, CAN ACCOMPLISH.

MICHELLE OBAMA

# YOU ARE YOUR OWN STORY, BLAZING THROUGH THE WORLD, TURNING HISTORY INTO HERSTORY.

NIKITA GILL

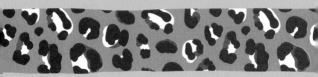

# NOTHING IS
# MIGHTIER
## THAN A WOMAN WHO KNOWS
# HER WORTH

I am here.
I am whole.
I am able.

ALEXANDRA ELLE

# MY MISSION IN LIFE IS NOT MERELY TO SURVIVE, BUT TO THRIVE.

MAYA ANGELOU

# STRONG WOMEN CELEBRATE EACH OTHER'S SUCCESS

# THE QUESTION ISN'T WHO'S GOING TO LET ME, IT'S WHO'S GOING TO STOP ME.

AYN RAND

Find a sense of self because with that, you can do anything else.

ANGELINA JOLIE

# THE WORLD NEEDS STRONG WOMEN WHO WILL LIFT AND BUILD OTHERS.

AMY TENNEY

THERE IS NO FORCE EQUAL TO A WOMAN DETERMINED TO RISE

ALWAYS, ALWAYS, ALWAYS BELIEVE IN YOURSELF. BECAUSE IF YOU DON'T, WHO WILL?

MARILYN MONROE

REALIZING THAT
YOU'RE NOT ALONE,
THAT YOU ARE
STANDING WITH
MILLIONS OF YOUR
SISTERS AROUND
THE WORLD IS VITAL.

MALALA YOUSAFZAI

**LIFE CHANGES WHEN YOU ALLOW ANOTHER WOMAN'S FIRE TO SPARK YOUR OWN**

# NO NEED TO BE ANYBODY BUT ONESELF.

VIRGINIA WOOLF

# NEVER CONSIDER OTHERS AS YOUR COMPETITION BECAUSE YOU ARE THE ONLY COMPETITOR OF YOURSELF.

SIMONE BILES

I believe in
being strong when
everything seems to
be going wrong.

AUDREY HEPBURN

# YOU HAVE MORE INNER STRENGTH THAN YOU REALIZE

**WORK HARD AT BEING THE BEST VERSION OF YOURSELF.**

ISADORA DUNCAN

I THINK THAT
WHEN WE
STAND IN
SOLIDARITY,
WE'LL BE
STRONGER.

IBTIHAJ MUHAMMAD

WHEN A WOMAN COLLABORATES WITH HER SISTERS,

THEY ARE STRONG ENOUGH TO SOLVE EVEN THE TOUGHEST PROBLEMS

I do my best,
and that's all
I can do.

CAROLINE WOZNIACKI

# WOMEN ARE EMPOWERED AND STRONG.

GAL GADOT

I'M PROUD
OF MYSELF.
I LIKE THE WAY
I'M MADE.

FREIDA PINTO

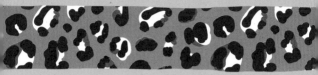

# NEVER
### APOLOGIZE FOR YOUR
# POWER

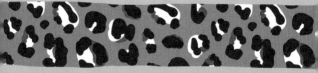

A STRONG WOMAN
IS A WOMAN
DETERMINED TO DO
SOMETHING OTHERS
ARE DETERMINED
NOT BE DONE.

MARGE PIERCY

# WOMEN DON'T NEED TO FIND THEIR VOICE, THEY NEED TO FEEL EMPOWERED TO USE IT.

MEGHAN, DUCHESS OF SUSSEX

# STRONG WOMEN DON'T POINT FINGERS, THEY STAND AND DEAL

# YOU ARE MORE POWERFUL THAN YOU KNOW.

MELISSA ETHERIDGE

*I know that
I am a woman,
a woman with inner
strength and a great
deal of courage!*

ANNE FRANK

# I BELIEVE IN THE IMPOSSIBLE BECAUSE NO ONE ELSE DOES.

FLORENCE GRIFFITH JOYNER

# A STRONG WOMAN PERSEVERES NO MATTER WHAT HAPPENS IN LIFE

IT ISN'T
WHAT WE SAY
OR THINK THAT
DEFINES US,
BUT WHAT
WE DO.

JANE AUSTEN

It's time to
take ownership in
our own success.

TORY BURCH

**STRONG WOMEN ARE CONFIDENT IN THEIR OWN ABILITY YET BRAVE ENOUGH TO ACCEPT SUPPORT WHEN NEEDED**

# MAY ALL YOUR VIBES SAY: I GOT THIS.

CLEO WADE

I LIKE TO PLAY A
STRONG WOMAN,
BUT A STRONG
WOMAN CAN
ALSO BE FRAGILE
AND VULNERABLE
AT THE SAME TIME.

CARICE VAN HOUTEN

# DON'T BE INTIMIDATED BY WHAT YOU DON'T KNOW; THAT CAN BE YOUR STRENGTH.

SARA BLAKELY

# BEHIND EVERY SUCCESSFUL WOMAN IS HER TRIBE OF SUPPORTING SISTERS

# EVERY WOMAN'S SUCCESS SHOULD BE AN INSPIRATION TO ANOTHER.

SERENA WILLIAMS

# THE LESS YOU REVEAL, THE MORE PEOPLE CAN WONDER.

EMMA WATSON

# NOTHING IS MORE EMPOWERING THAN A WOMAN WHO

## CHAMPIONS HERSELF YET STILL CELEBRATES OTHER WOMEN

You don't
have to play
masculine to be a
strong woman.

MARY ELIZABETH
WINSTEAD

# I DON'T THINK THERE IS ANYTHING WRONG WITH JUST QUIETLY BELIEVING IN YOURSELF.

JESSICA ENNIS-HILL

WOMEN HAVE
ALWAYS BEEN
THE STRONG
ONES OF THE
WORLD.

COCO CHANEL

# NEVER
## APOLOGIZE FOR SETTING
# HEALTHY
## BOUNDARIES

We need to
reshape our own
perception of how
we view ourselves.

BEYONCÉ

# WOMEN SHOULD NEVER BE AFRAID TO REACH FOR THE STARS.

CATHERINE RENIER

TURN A "CAN'T" INTO A "CAN" AND TURN YOUR DREAMS INTO PLANS

# IT'S NOT WHERE YOU COME FROM; IT'S WHERE YOU'RE HEADING.

DEBORAH MEADEN

WE HAVE TO LIFT
EACH OTHER UP,
NOT TRY TO CLAW
EACH OTHER DOWN.

ARIANA GRANDE

# BE HAPPY WITH WHO YOU ARE, AND NOT WHO PEOPLE THINK YOU ARE.

KARREN BRADY

I AM ME.
NOTHING MORE,
NOTHING LESS
AND THAT
IS ENOUGH

# WHAT MAKES YOU DIFFERENT OR WEIRD, THAT'S YOUR STRENGTH.

MERYL STREEP

Don't
compromise
yourself.

JANIS JOPLIN

# YOU MOVE DIFFERENT WHEN YOU UNDERSTAND YOUR POWER

**IF SOMEONE ASKS ME SOMETHING THAT I REALLY DON'T WANT TO DO, I SAY NO.**

DIANA ROSS

YOU BECOME
STRONG BY
DOING THE
THING YOU
NEED TO BE
STRONG FOR.

AUDRE LORDE

You can do
anything you
decide to do.

AMELIA EARHART

# BE THE WOMAN YOU LOOK UP TO

I AM THE SOLE AUTHOR OF THE DICTIONARY THAT DEFINES ME.

ZADIE SMITH

# WOMEN ARE THE REAL ARCHITECTS OF SOCIETY.

CHER

# A STRONG WOMAN MAY FEEL THE FEAR

# BUT WALKS FORWARD REGARDLESS

ANY TIME WOMEN COME TOGETHER WITH A COLLECTIVE INTENTION, IT'S A POWERFUL THING.

PHYLICIA RASHAD

# THERE'S NO LIMIT
# TO WHAT I CAN DO.

### LEYLAH FERNANDEZ

# THINK LIKE A QUEEN. A QUEEN IS NOT AFRAID TO FAIL.

OPRAH WINFREY

# STRONG WOMEN
## TREAT OBSTACLES AS
# STEPPING STONES
## ON THEIR WAY TO
# SUCCESS

In a world where so many yearn to be liked, I'd rather be respected.

SAMANTHA
KING HOLMES

# I DON'T LIKE DEFINING MYSELF. I JUST AM.

BRITNEY SPEARS

# A WOMAN IS UNSTOPPABLE WHEN SHE REALIZES SHE DESERVES THE BEST

# FIND OUT WHO YOU ARE AND DO IT ON PURPOSE.

DOLLY PARTON

You can
control your
response to your
circumstances.

CONDOLEEZZA RICE

# IF THERE'S ONE THING I'VE LEARNED IN LIFE, IT'S THE POWER OF USING YOUR VOICE.

MICHELLE OBAMA

BE THAT WOMAN
WHO ROOTS FOR
HERSELF AND
ENCOURAGES
OTHER WOMEN
TO BELIEVE IN
THEMSELVES

# EMBRACE
# WHAT MAKES
# YOU UNIQUE.

JANELLE MONÁE

WHEN YOU
SEE
SOMETHING
YOU ADMIRE IN
ANOTHER WOMAN,
TELL HER

# IT'S THE MOMENT YOU THINK YOU CAN'T, THAT YOU CAN.

CELINE DION

# BE YOUR OWN DEFINITION OF AMAZING.

NIKITA GILL

Speak your mind,
even if your
voice shakes.

RUTH BADER GINSBURG

# THERE IS NOTHING STRONGER THAN A WOMAN WHO REBUILT HERSELF

# WOMEN
## ARE
## FIERCE.

LANG LEAV

# SOMETIMES YOU HAVE TO REALIZE THAT YOU'VE HAD ENOUGH TO REALIZE THAT YOU ARE ENOUGH.

MANDY HALE

# NOTHING IS MIGHTIER THAN A WOMAN WHO

## DOES NOT SEEK THE VALIDATION OF ANYONE BUT HERSELF

I'm worthy enough, beautiful enough and I don't need anybody else to feel whole.

DEMI LOVATO

# A STRONG WOMAN IS BOTH SOFT AND POWERFUL.

RITU GHATOUREY

# I DO BELIEVE
# IN THE STRENGTH
# OF WOMEN.

KATY PERRY

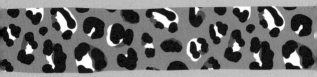

BEING
**COMFORTABLE**
IN YOUR OWN SKIN
**IS PRICELESS**

EMPOWERING WOMEN DOESN'T COME FROM SELFISHNESS BUT RATHER FROM SELFLESSNESS.

SELENE KINDER

# IT IS IMPORTANT TO BE FEARLESS YET VULNERABLE. IT TAKES COURAGE TO DO BOTH.

NICOLE SCHERZINGER

# YOU ARE A
# SUPERHERO

WE ALL MOVE
FORWARD WHEN
WE REALIZE
HOW RESILIENT
AND STRIKING
THE WOMEN
AROUND US ARE.

RUPI KAUR

Confidence

empowers you.

SIMONE BILES

I DON'T WANT
OTHER PEOPLE TO
DECIDE WHAT I AM.
I WANT TO DECIDE
THAT FOR MYSELF.

EMMA WATSON

# ALWAYS REMEMBER THAT YOU ARE WORTHY.

CLEO WADE

You can carve
your own path,
be your own
kind of leader.

JACINDA ARDERN

# STRONG WOMEN SLAY THEIR GOALS AND LEAVE A GLOW ON OTHER WOMEN

# IT'S ALL ABOUT HAVING THAT INNER CONFIDENCE.

JENNIFER ANISTON

# YOU CAN BE
# DEFIANT AND
# REBELLIOUS AND
# STILL BE STRONG
# AND POSITIVE.

MADONNA

# BE HAPPY WITH THE BEAUTIFUL THINGS THAT MAKE YOU, YOU.

BEYONCÉ

HAVING
THE RIGHT
CIRCLE OF
WOMEN
AROUND
YOU IS THE
BIGGEST
LIFE
UPGRADE

# I AM SHOWING UP FOR ALL THE TIMES I THOUGHT I COULDN'T.

ALEXANDRA ELLE

# I AM SIMPLY A STRONG WOMAN AND KNOW MY WORTH.

ANGELINA JOLIE

# BE THE
# HEROINE OF
# YOUR OWN
# LIFE STORY

*Overpower.*
*Overtake.*
*Overcome.*

SERENA WILLIAMS

# IT'S PRETTY INCREDIBLE TO SEE WHAT HAPPENS WHEN YOU START BELIEVING YOU ARE ENOUGH.

MEGHAN, DUCHESS OF SUSSEX

HAVING A
SOFT HEART
IN A CRUEL
WORLD IS
**COURAGE, NOT
WEAKNESS.**

KATHERINE HENSON

ONE WOMAN CAN MAKE
A DIFFERENCE,
BUT TOGETHER WE CAN
ROCK THE WORLD

Life is tough,
my darling, but
so are you.

STEPHANIE BENNETT-HENRY

A REALLY STRONG WOMAN ACCEPTS THE WAR SHE WENT THROUGH AND IS ENNOBLED BY HER SCARS.

CARLY SIMON

STRONG WOMEN DON'T WAIT FOR OPPORTUNITIES, THEY MAKE THEM

I THINK THE
KEY FOR WOMEN
IS NOT TO SET
ANY LIMITS.

MARTINA NAVRATILOVA

# BE LIKE A SINGLE FLOWER, NOT A WHOLE BOUQUET.

ANNA HELD

# EACH TIME A WOMAN STANDS UP FOR HERSELF... SHE STANDS UP FOR ALL WOMEN.

MAYA ANGELOU

# YOU ARE NEVER TOO SMALL TO MAKE A DIFFERENCE.

GRETA THUNBERG

Believe in
yourself when
no one else does —
that makes you a
winner right there.

VENUS WILLIAMS

A STRONG WOMAN SAYS "I'M GREAT AND SO IS SHE" INSTEAD OF "I'M BETTER THAN HER"

# OWN YOURSELF,
# WOMAN.

TONI MORRISON

# BE TOUGH ENOUGH TO FOLLOW THROUGH.

ROSALYNN CARTER

We realize the importance of our voices only when we are silenced.

MALALA YOUSAFZAI

# NEVER APOLOGIZE FOR BEING AN AMBITIOUS, CONFIDENT, STRONG-MINDED WOMAN

WE ARE
STRONG,
BUT
TOGETHER
WE ARE
UNSTOPPABLE.

WENDY AIMEE PORTER

# I KNOW MY WORTH. I EMBRACE MY POWER.

AMY SCHUMER

# A STRONG WOMAN WORKS

# ON HERSELF, BY HERSELF, FOR HERSELF

I CAN DO
ANYTHING.
I AM STRONG.
I AM INVINCIBLE.
I AM WOMAN.

HELEN REDDY

# I WANT TO BE TRUE TO WHO I AM.

ANNIE LENNOX

# SOME OF YOUR GREATEST PAINS BECOME YOUR GREATEST STRENGTHS.

DREW BARRYMORE

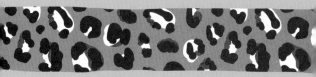

# IN A WORLD
## WHERE YOU CAN
## BE ANYTHING, YOUR
# GREATEST POWER
## IS TO BE YOURSELF

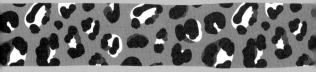

I will stand
fiercely in my
power and
claim my joy.

ALEXANDRA ELLE

# I'M STRONGER THAN I THINK I AM.

MISTY MAY-TREANOR

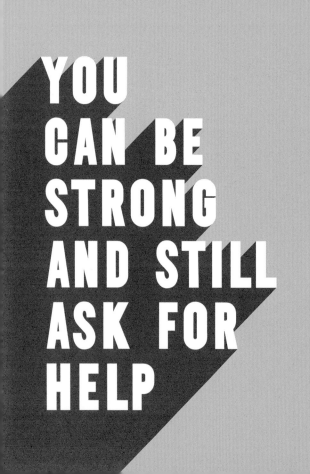

YOU CAN BE STRONG AND STILL ASK FOR HELP

# YOU MUST BELIEVE IN YOURSELF.

CHER

Women are
the largest untapped
reservoir of talent
in the world.

HILLARY CLINTON

ONE OF
THE MOST
COURAGEOUS
THINGS YOU
CAN DO IS
IDENTIFY
YOURSELF.

SHEILA MURRAY BETHEL

YOU ARE STRONG
ENOUGH TO HANDLE
YOUR CHALLENGES,
WISE ENOUGH TO
FIND SOLUTIONS TO
YOUR PROBLEMS.

LORI DESCHENE

ONCE YOU FIGURE OUT WHAT RESPECT TASTES LIKE, IT TASTES BETTER THAN ATTENTION.

P!NK

BEHIND EVERY STRONG WOMAN THERE IS ANOTHER WHISPERING "YOU'VE GOT THIS" IN HER EAR

# YOU ARE
# BEAUTIFUL JUST
# AS YOU ARE.

MELISSA ETHERIDGE

# AT THE END OF THE DAY, WE CAN ENDURE MUCH MORE THAN WE THINK WE CAN.

FRIDA KAHLO

Womanhood
is you.

VIOLA DAVIS

EMPOWERED
WOMEN
EMPOWER
WOMEN

# YOU ARE POWERFUL AND YOUR VOICE MATTERS.

KAMALA HARRIS

WHERE
THERE IS A
WOMAN,
THERE IS
MAGIC.

NTOZAKE SHANGE

Have you enjoyed this book? If so, find us
on Facebook at Summersdale Publishers,
on Twitter at @Summersdale and on
Instagram at @summersdalebooks and
get in touch. We'd love to hear from you!

www.summersdale.com

**Image credits**

Leopard icon throughout © Nadia Grapes/Shutterstock.
com; Leopard print pattern on pp.3, 6, 9, 12, 22, 25, 27, 35,
37, 47, 48, 50, 60, 63, 69, 72, 75, 85, 88, 90, 98, 100, 110, 111,
113, 123, 126, 132, 135, 138, 148, 151, 153, 160 © Sandra_M/
Shutterstock.com; Leopard print pattern on pp.7, 17, 19, 32,
38, 44, 57, 59, 70, 80, 82, 95, 101, 107, 120, 122, 133, 143,
145, 158 © Sinichka/Shutterstock.com; Paw print shape
throughout © Creative icon styles/Shutterstock.com